SRA
Open Court Reading

Book 2

Keep Trying

•

Being Afraid

•

Homes

SRA Open Court Reading

Book 2

Program Authors

Marilyn Jager Adams

Carl Bereiter

Anne McKeough

Robbie Case

Marsha Roit

Jan Hirshberg

Michael Pressley

Iva Carruthers

Gerald H. Treadway, Jr.

SRA

A Division of The McGraw-Hill Companies

Columbus, Ohio

Acknowledgments

Grateful acknowledgment is given to the following publishers and copyright owners for permissions granted to reprint selections from their publications. All possible care has been taken to trace ownership and secure permission for each selection included.

Baynard Presse International: "The Rabbit Warren" by Marie Aubinais, illustrated by Monique Félix from *Pomme d'Api*.

Candlewick Press Inc.: **"The Cat and the Mice" and "The Hare and the Tortoise" from THE BEST OF AESOP'S FABLES Text Copyright © 1990 Margaret Clark. Illustrations Copyright © 1990 Charlotte Voake. Reproduced by permission of the publisher Candlewick Press Inc., Cambridge, MA.**

The Child's World, Inc.: "Make a Home" from ANIMAL HABITATS: THE BEST HOME OF ALL by Nancy Pemberton, illustrations by Barbara Bruno. Copyright © 1990 by The Child's World, Inc. Reprinted with permission of The Child's World, Inc.

Children's Press, Inc.: ANIMAL HOMES by Illa Podendorf. Copyright © 1991 by Children's Press, Inc. Reprinted with permission of Children's Press, Inc.

Clarion Books/Houghton Mifflin Co.: THE LITTLE RED HEN by Paul Galdone. Copyright © 1973 by Paul Galdone. Reprinted by permission of Clarion Books/Houghton Mifflin Co. All rights reserved.

Dutton Children's Books, a division of Penguin Putnam Inc.: From CLYDE MONSTER by Robert L. Crowe, Illustrated by Kay Chorao. Copyright © 1976 by Robert L. Crowe, text. Copyright © 1976 by Kay Sproat Chorao, illustrations. Used by permission of Dutton Children's Books, a division of Penguin Putnam Inc.

Farrar, Straus & Giroux, Inc.: THE THREE LITTLE PIGS by Margot Zemach. Copyright © 1989 by Margot Zemach. Reprinted by permission of Farrar, Strauss & Giroux, Inc.

Golden Books Publishing, Company, Inc.: HOME FOR A BUNNY by Margaret Wise Brown, Illustrated by Garth Williams © 1956 Golden Books Publishing Company, Inc. All rights reserved. Reprinted by permission.

Greenwillow Books, a division of William Morrow & Company, Inc.: BUILDING A HOUSE by Byron Barton. Copyright © 1981 by Byron Barton. By permission of Greenwillow Books, a division of William Morrow & Company Inc.

HarperCollins Publishers: "THE GARDEN" from FROG AND TOAD TOGETHER by ARNOLD LOBEL COPYRIGHT © 1971, 1972 BY ARNOLD LOBEL. Used by permission of HarperCollins Publishers. "GOBLIN STORY" from LITTLE BEAR'S VISIT by ELSE HOLMELUND MINARIK, illustrations by MAURICE SENDAK. Used by permission of HarperCollins Publishers. "THE KITE" from DAYS WITH FROG AND TOAD by ARNOLD LOBEL. COPYRIGHT © 1979 by ARNOLD LOBEL. Used by permission of HarperCollins Publishers. "STRANGE BUMPS" from OWL AT HOME by ARNOLD LOBEL. Used by permission of HarperCollins Publishers.

Little, Brown and Company: "The Cat and the Mice" and "The Hare and the Tortoise" from THE BEST OF AESOP'S FABLES by Margaret Clark. Copyright © 1990 by Margaret Clark (text); copyright © 1990 by Charlotte Voake (illustrations). By permission of Little, Brown and Company.

The Estate of Kazue Mizumura: THE WAY OF AN ANT by Kazue Mizumura. Copyright © 1970 by Kazue Mizumura. Reprinted with permission of The Estate of Kazue Mizumura.

Multimedia Product Development, Inc.:*My Brother is Afraid of Just About Everything* by Lois Osborn. Copyright © 1982. Reprinted by permission of Multimedia Product Development, Inc., Chicago, IL.

Orchard Books: **From IS THIS A HOUSE FOR HERMIT CRAB? by Megan McDonald, illustrated by S.D. Schindler. Text copyright © 1990 by Megan McDonald, illustration copyright © by S.D. Schindler. Reprinted by permission of Orchard Books, New York.**

Marian Reiner: "74TH Street" from THE MALIBU AND OTHER POEMS by Myra Cohn Livingston. Copyright © 1972 by Myra Cohn Livingston. Reprinted by permission of Marian Reiner.

Scholastic Inc.: *"Something is There" from SPOOKY RHYMES AND RIDDLES by Lilian Moore. Copyright © 1972 by Lilian Moore. Reprinted by permission of Scholastic Inc.*

SRA/McGraw-Hill

A Division of The McGraw·Hill Companies

Send all inquiries to:
SRA/McGraw-Hill
8787 Orion Place
Columbus, Ohio 43240-4027

Printed in the United States of America.

ISBN 0-02-830951-0

4 5 6 7 8 9 RRD 04 03 02 01 00

Program Authors

Marilyn Jager Adams, Ph.D.
BBN Technologies

Carl Bereiter, Ph.D.
University of Toronto

Anne McKeough, Ph.D.
University of Toronto

Robbie Case, Ph.D.
University of Toronto

Marsha Roit, Ph.D.
National Reading Consultant

Jan Hirshberg, Ed.D.

Michael Pressley, Ph.D.
University of Notre Dame

Iva Carruthers, Ph.D.
Northeastern Illinois University

Gerald H. Treadway, Jr., Ed.D.
San Diego State University

Table *of* Contents

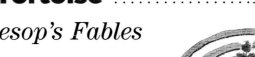

Table *of* Contents

Table *of* Contents

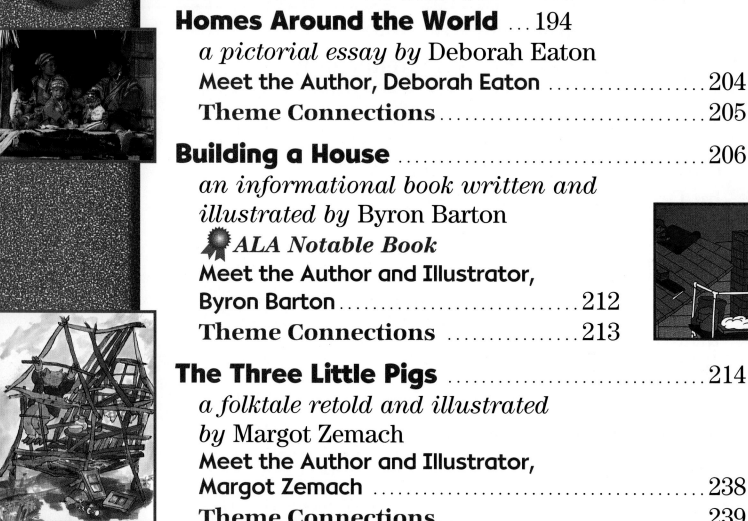

Keep Trying

Have you ever tried very, very hard to learn something new or maybe to build something? Was it hard to learn to ride a bike or to roller skate? Did you keep trying until you finally learned? How did it feel?

They didn't
give up!

The Little Red Hen

retold and illustrated by Paul Galdone

Once upon a time a cat and a dog and a mouse and a little red hen all lived together in a cozy little house.

The cat liked to sleep all day on the soft couch.

The dog liked to nap all day on the sunny back porch.

And the mouse liked to snooze all day in the warm chair by the fireside.

So the little red hen had to do all the housework.

She cooked the meals and washed the dishes and made the beds. She swept the floor and washed the windows and mended the clothes.

She raked the leaves and mowed the grass and hoed the garden.

One day when she was hoeing the
garden she found some grains of wheat.
"Who will plant this wheat?" cried the
little red hen.

"Not I," said the cat.

"Not I," said the dog.

"Not I," said the mouse.

"Then I will," said the little red hen.
And she did.

Each morning the little red hen
watered the wheat and pulled the weeds.
Soon the wheat pushed through the
ground and began to grow tall.

When the wheat was ripe, the little red hen asked, "Who will cut this wheat?"

"NOT I," said the cat.

"NOT I," said the dog.

"NOT I," said the mouse.

"Then I will," said the little red hen. And she did.

When the wheat was all cut, the little
red hen asked, "Now, who will take this
wheat to the mill to be ground into flour?"

"Not I," said the cat.

"Not I," said the dog.

"Not I," said the mouse.

"Then I will," said the little red hen.
And she did.

The little red hen returned from the mill carrying a small bag of fine white flour.

"Who will make a cake from this fine white flour?" asked the little red hen.

"Not I," said the cat.

"Not I," said the dog.

"Not I," said the mouse.

"Then I will," said the little red hen.
And she did.

She gathered sticks and made a fire in the stove. Then she took milk and sugar and eggs and butter and mixed them in a big bowl with the fine white flour.

When the oven was hot she poured the cake batter into a shining pan and put it in the oven.

Soon a delicious smell filled the cozy little house.

The cat got off the soft couch and strolled into the kitchen.

The dog got up from the sunny back porch and came into the kitchen.

The mouse jumped down from his warm chair and scampered into the kitchen.

The little red hen was just taking a
beautiful cake out of the oven.

"Who will eat this cake?" asked the little red hen.

"I WILL!" cried the cat.

"I WILL!" cried the dog.

"I WILL!" cried the mouse.

But the little red hen said, "All by myself I planted the wheat, I tended the wheat, I cut the wheat, I took the wheat to the mill to be ground into flour.

All by myself I gathered the sticks, I built the fire, I mixed the cake. And all by myself I am going to eat it!"

And so she did, to the very last crumb.

After that, whenever there was work to be done, the little red hen had three very eager helpers.

The Little Red Hen

Meet the Author and Illustrator

Paul Galdone was born in Hungary. He moved to the United States when he was 14. He did not speak English, so he had to go to three English classes a day. When Paul was older, he went to art school. He then got a job where he designed book jackets. He loved illustrating and went on to make his own picture book.

Theme Connections

Talk About It

Pick a partner and talk about these questions.

- Why didn't the other animals help the Little Red Hen?
- Should the Little Red Hen share with the other animals?
- Why or why not?
- What lesson does this story teach?

Look at the Concept/Question Board. Are there any questions on it that you can answer now? Do you have any new questions about trying? Write the questions on the Board. The next reading may help answer your questions.

Record Ideas

 Take out your Writing Journal. Design a book jacket for the story. Remember to add the title.

Share with Classmates

Share the book jackets with the class. Set them around the classroom for everyone to see.

The Kite

by Arnold Lobel

rog and Toad went out to fly a kite.
They went to a large meadow
where the wind was strong.

"Our kite will fly up and up," said Frog.
"It will fly all the way up to the top of
the sky."

"Toad," said Frog, "I will hold the ball
of string. You hold the kite and run."

Toad ran across the meadow.
He ran as fast as his short legs
could carry him.
The kite went up in the air.
It fell to the ground with a bump.

Toad heard laughter.
Three robins were sitting in a bush.
"That kite will not fly," said the robins.
"You may as well give up."

Toad ran back to Frog.
"Frog," said Toad,
"this kite will not fly.
I give up."

"We must make a second try,"
said Frog. "Wave the kite
over your head. Perhaps
that will make it fly."

Toad ran back
across the meadow.
He waved the kite
over his head.
The kite went up in the air
and then fell down with a thud.

"What a joke!" said the robins.
"That kite will never
get off the ground."

Toad ran back to Frog.
"This kite is a joke," he said.
"It will never get off the ground."

"We have to make
a third try," said Frog.
"Wave the kite over your head
and jump up and down.
Perhaps that will make it fly."

Toad ran across the meadow again.
He waved the kite over his head.
He jumped up and down.
The kite went up in the air and
crashed down into the grass.

"That kite is junk,"
said the robins.
"Throw it away and go home."

Toad ran back to Frog.
"This kite is junk," he said.
"I think we should throw it
away and go home."

"Toad," said Frog,
"we need one more try.
Wave the kite over your head.
Jump up and down
and shout UP KITE UP."
    Toad ran across the meadow.
He waved the kite over his head.
He jumped up and down.
He shouted, "UP KITE UP!"

The kite flew into the air.
It climbed higher and higher.

"We did it!" cried Toad.
"Yes," said Frog.
"If a running try
did not work,
and a running and waving try
did not work,
and a running, waving,
and jumping try
did not work,

I knew that
a running, waving, jumping,
and shouting try
just had to work."

The robins flew out of the bush.
But they could not fly as high
as the kite.

Frog and Toad sat and watched their kite. It seemed to be flying way up at the top of the sky.

The Garden

by Arnold Lobel

Frog was in his garden. Toad came walking by. "What a fine garden you have, Frog," he said.

"Yes," said Frog. "It is very nice, but it was hard work."

"I wish I had a garden," said Toad.

"Here are some flower seeds. Plant them in the ground," said Frog, "and soon you will have a garden."

"How soon?" asked Toad.

"Quite soon," said Frog.

Toad ran home. He planted the flower seeds. "Now seeds," said Toad, "start growing."

Toad walked up and down a few times.
The seeds did not start to grow. Toad put
his head close to the ground and said
loudly, "Now seeds, start growing!"

Toad looked at the ground again. The seeds did not start to grow. Toad put his head very close to the ground and shouted, "NOW SEEDS, START GROWING!"

Frog came running up the path. "What is all this noise?" he asked.

"My seeds will not grow," said Toad.

"You are shouting too much," said Frog. "These poor seeds are afraid to grow."

"My seeds are afraid to grow?" asked Toad.

"Of course," said Frog. "Leave them alone for a few days. Let the sun shine on them, let the rain fall on them. Soon your seeds will start to grow."

That night Toad looked out of his window. "Drat!" said Toad. "My seeds have not started to grow. They must be afraid of the dark."

Toad went out to his garden with some candles. "I will read the seeds a story," said Toad. "Then they will not be afraid."

Toad read a long story to his seeds.

All the next day Toad sang songs to his seeds.

And all the next day Toad read poems
to his seeds.

And all the next day Toad played
music for his seeds.

Toad looked at the ground. The seeds
still did not start to grow.

"What shall I do?" cried Toad. "These must be the most frightened seeds in the whole world!"

Then Toad felt very tired, and he fell asleep.

"Toad, Toad, wake up," said Frog.
"Look at your garden!"

Toad looked at his garden. Little green plants were coming up out of the ground.

"At last," shouted Toad, "my seeds
have stopped being afraid to grow!"

"And now you will have a nice garden
too," said Frog.

"Yes," said Toad, "but you were right, Frog. It was very hard work."

The Garden

Meet the Author and Illustrator

Arnold Lobel was a daydreamer. When he was a child, he wrote stories and drew pictures for his classmates. He loved to hear Mother Goose stories. When he grew up, Arnold illustrated his favorite Mother Goose rhymes.

Theme Connections

Talk About It

Point out that there are different ways to keep trying as seen in the selections that have been read so far. Here are some things to talk about:

- How was the way the Little Red Hen kept trying different than the way Toad kept trying?
- Why did Toad sing and read and play music to his seeds?
- Did all those things help the seeds grow?

Look at the Concept/Question Board and answer any questions that you can. Do you have any new questions about trying? Write them on the Board. Maybe the next reading will help answer your questions.

Record Ideas

Print this question and your answer in your

 Writing Journal:

- What is something you had to try hard to learn to do?

Share with Other Classmates

Ask a classmate the same question that you answered in your Writing Journal. Talk about how your answers are the same and how they are different.

74th Street

Myra Cohn Livingston
illustrated by Stella Ormai

Hey, this little kid gets roller skates.
She puts them on.
She stands up and almost
flops over backwards.
She sticks out a foot like
she's going somewhere and
falls down and
smacks her hand. She
grabs hold of a step to get up and

sticks out the other foot and
slides about six inches and
falls and
skins her knee.

And then, you know what?

She brushes off the dirt and the
blood and puts some
spit on it and then
sticks out the other foot

again.

FINE Art

First Steps. 1943. **Pablo Picasso.** Oil on canvas. Gift of
Stephen C. Clark, B.A., 1903, Yale University Art Gallery.
©1999 Estate of Pablo Picasso/Artist Rights Society (ARS),
New York. Photo: Francis G. Mayer/Corbis.

Waiting. c. 1882.
Edgar Degas.
Pastel on paper.
19 × 24 in. Jointly
owned by the
Norton Simon
Art Foundation,
Pasadena,
California and the
J. Paul Getty
Museum, Malibu,
California.

***Study for the Munich Olympic
Games Poster.*** 1971. **Jacob
Lawrence.** Gouache on paper. The
Seattle Art Museum, purchased with
funds from P.O.N.C.H.O.

The Way Of An Ant

Kazue Mizumura

illustrated by Laurel Aiello

Once there was a young ant
who wanted to climb
as high as the blue sky.
He started to climb
the tallest blade of grass he could find.

When he reached the tip of the grass,
he looked up, and saw that a dandelion
stood even higher.
He raced down to the ground and started
to climb up the dandelion.

When he reached the top of the dandelion,
he looked up, and there against the sky
he saw a rose,
stretching its stem as high as it could go.
He hurried down to the ground and started
to climb up the stem of the rose.

When he reached the rose,
he stopped awhile to smell its petals.
Then he thought he saw the sun in the sky.
But it was only a sunflower's
golden ring, shining
high above the rose.
He tumbled down to the ground and started
to climb up the sunflower.

When he reached the face of the sunflower,
a gnarled branch of an apple tree
with three green apples
hung over him.
He quickly ran down to the ground and started
to climb up the apple tree.

When he reached the top of the apple tree,
he looked up and saw a maple tree
shading him from the sky with
its fanlike leaves.
He rushed down to the ground and started
to climb up the maple tree.

When he reached the top of the maple
tree, he took a deep breath
and looked around for the sky.
But there was an enormous oak tree
towering over the whole field.
He ran down to the ground,
dashed across the field, and started
to climb up the oak tree.

When he reached the top of the oak tree,
he was very tired.
But the higher he climbed,
the higher he wanted to climb.

Then he saw a pine tree
on a faraway hilltop
reaching up to the sky.
He went down again to the ground,
ran to the hilltop, and started
to climb the pine tree.

When he reached the top of the pine tree,
there was the blue sky as far as he could see.
And there were mountains beyond mountains
and trees beyond trees,
enough for him to climb forever.

At last he understood.
As long as he kept on climbing,
the blue sky grew higher and higher.

He slowly turned his head
and looked behind him.

And there he saw
the pine tree
the oak tree
the maple tree
the apple tree
the sunflower
the rose
the dandelion
and the grass.

How surprised he was to see
how hard he had tried.
How happy he was to have
climbed so high.

But now he was much older
and a little wiser, and
he would climb no more.

He started down,
and on the way he met a young ant
rushing and puffing to climb up to
the sky.
The old ant smiled and nodded
at the young ant, and passed
without saying a word.

The Way Of An Ant

Meet the Author

Kazue Mizumura began her career as an illustrator. Her interest in art began as a child living in Japan. "I always liked to draw and that was the only thing I could do really well . . . [in] school." After she moved to the United States, she was encouraged to write her own stories. Now she writes and illustrates her own books.

Meet the Illustrator

Laurel Aiello has illustrated for textbooks, party books, cookbooks, and storybooks. She says of this particular story, "Since I have always liked to draw animals, I found it especially fun to illustrate this story about an adventurous ant. I tried to make him 'come alive' for you as he travels through the world of grass, flowers and trees."

Theme Connections

Talk About It

Ant kept trying to reach the sky. Here are some questions to think and talk about.

- Why did the ant want to climb as high as the sky?
- What do you think it would look like?
- Has anyone ever been to the sky?

Look at the Concept/Question Board. Are there any questions on it that you can answer now? Do you have any new questions about trying? Maybe the next reading will help answer your questions.

Record Ideas

 Draw a picture in your Writing Journal of what you think you would see if you climbed as high as the sky. Print and answer the following question in your journal: What lesson does this story teach about trying?

Tell a Story to Other Classmates

Join a group of your classmates. Imagine you are going on a rocket ship and you are trying to fly as high as the sky. Listen to the stories of your classmates.

The Fox and the Grapes

Aesop

illustrated by Judith Moffatt

One day a fox was running down a dusty road. He was hot and thirsty. Soon he saw some grapes hanging on a vine in a garden.

The grapes were large and ripe and juicy. They looked very tasty to the hot, thirsty fox.

"How I wish I had some of those grapes," said the fox.

The fox jumped high in the air.
He reached up with his paw, but
he did not get the grapes.

He jumped higher and higher,
but he still could not get the
grapes.

At last the fox gave up.

"Those grapes can stay on the vine," said the fox. "I can tell that they are sour. They must taste awful. I don't like sour grapes."

The Hare and the Tortoise

from THE BEST OF AESOP'S FABLES
Aesop
retold by Margaret Clark
illustrated by Charlotte Voake

A hare was one day making fun of a tortoise. "You are a slowpoke," he said. "You couldn't run if you tried."

"Don't laugh at me," said the tortoise. "I bet that I could beat you in a race."

"Couldn't," replied the hare.

"Could," replied the tortoise.

"All right," said the hare. "I'll race you. But I'll win, even with my eyes shut."

They asked a passing fox to set them off.

"Ready, set, go!" said the fox.

The hare went off at a great pace. He got
so far ahead he decided he might as well
stop for a rest. Soon he fell fast asleep.

The tortoise came plodding along,
never stopping for a moment.

When the hare woke up, he ran as fast as he could to the finish line.

But he was too late—the tortoise had already won the race!

The Hare and the Tortoise

Meet the Authors

Aesop lived nearly 3,000 years ago in Greece. He was known for teaching people by telling funny little stories. Aesop remembered hundreds of these stories, yet he never wrote any of them down. The stories he told are still popular today.

Margaret Clark began to write stories for her children when they were very little. Her children and her stories grew up together. Clark likes to write about things she has done, like camping, but has also retold stories done by other people, such as Aesop, in a new way.

Meet the Illustrator

Charlotte Voake always wanted to be an illustrator. She won a poster contest when she was twelve. She published her first book while she was still in college. She lives in England and enjoys sailing when she isn't drawing.

Theme Connections

Think About It

This well-known folktale contains a simple but powerful message. Here are some questions to help you think about the story.

- Which animal can run faster—the hare or the tortoise?
- Why did the tortoise win?
- Why did the hare go to sleep during the race?

Look at the Concept/Question Board. Are there any questions on it that you can answer now? Do you have any new questions about trying? Write the questions on the Board. Maybe the next reading will help answer your questions.

Record Ideas

 Take out your Writing Journal and print this question in it: "What lesson does this story teach about trying?" Then print your answer.

Share with a Classmate

Share with a classmate what you wrote in your Writing Journal about the story's lesson. Then listen to what your classmate wrote. Talk about how your Writing Journal entries are the same and how they are different.

Bibliography

Amazing Grace

by Mary Hoffman. Grace's determination to be Peter Pan will amaze you.

Flap Your Wings and Try

by Charlotte Pomerantz. Let a baby sea gull give you a hint about success.

Fox on the Job

by James Marshall. Fox needs a new bike and that means he has to get a job.

The Gardener

by Sarah Stewart. When Lydia Grace's father loses his job, she goes to live with Uncle Jim in the city. Find out how she plants a garden in a very unusual place.

Katy and the Big Snow

by Virginia Burton. How does Katy the tractor save the day?

Little Toot

by Hardie Gramatky. This little tugboat becomes a hero during a storm.

Mirette on the High Wire

by Emily Arnold McCully. Join Mirette, high above Paris, when she learns to walk the high wire.

Sing, Sophie!

by Dayle Ann Dodds. Something is scarier than Sophie's singing. What could it be?

Being Afraid

Being afraid is not fun, but everyone is afraid sometimes. What do you do when you are afraid? What do your friends do? The story characters you will meet in this unit find many different things to be afraid of and many different ways to act when they are afraid. See how they feel about being afraid.

My Brother Is Afraid Of Just About Everything

Lois Osborn
illustrated by Loretta Krupinski

My little brother is afraid of just about everything. Whenever there's a thunderstorm, I know where to find him.

Underneath the bed.

When we're outside and the mailman
comes, I know where to find him.
Behind the bushes.
He doesn't like men with beards.

When he's in the bathtub, he
screams if I let the water out. Maybe
he thinks he'll go down the drain along
with the water.

So I take him out first. Then I empty
the tub.

Yesterday my mother started to vacuum. My brother started to howl. Maybe he thinks the vacuum cleaner is a monster. He sure acts that way.

So my mother asked me to take him for a walk.

We went past my school. "See?" I said. "That's where you'll be going in a couple of years."

I could tell by my brother's face what
he thought about *that.*

We met some of my friends at the playground. They think my brother is cute. "What's your name?" and "How old are you?" they asked.

Did my brother answer them?
No-o-o, of course not.
He just buried his face in my
stomach, the way he always does.

On our way home, we came to some railroad tracks. A train was coming, so we waited to cross.

Most kids think trains are pretty exciting. They wave at the engineer. They count cars. But not my brother.

His arms went around me like
boa constrictors. I couldn't have
shaken him loose if I'd wanted to.

Back home, we sat together under the big tree in our backyard. I decided it was time we had a talk.

"Look," I said to him, "did thunder and lightning ever hurt you?" He shook his head.

"Or the mailman, or the vacuum cleaner?" He shook his head again.

"Then how come you're so scared of everything?" I asked.

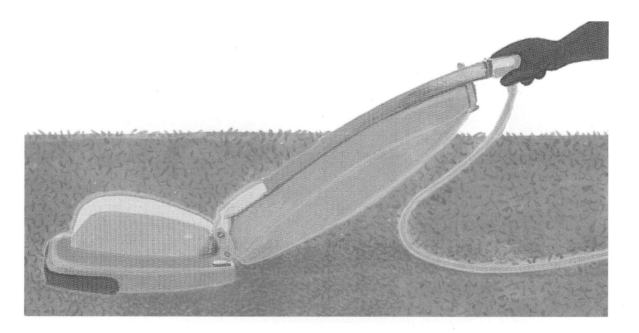

My brother's face drooped. The corners of his mouth turned down and quivered. His shoulders came up to his ears. His big eyes looked at me.

I felt like patting him on the back and saying that everything was okay.

But instead I said, "Look, you've got to get tough. It's stupid to keep on being afraid of things that won't hurt you."

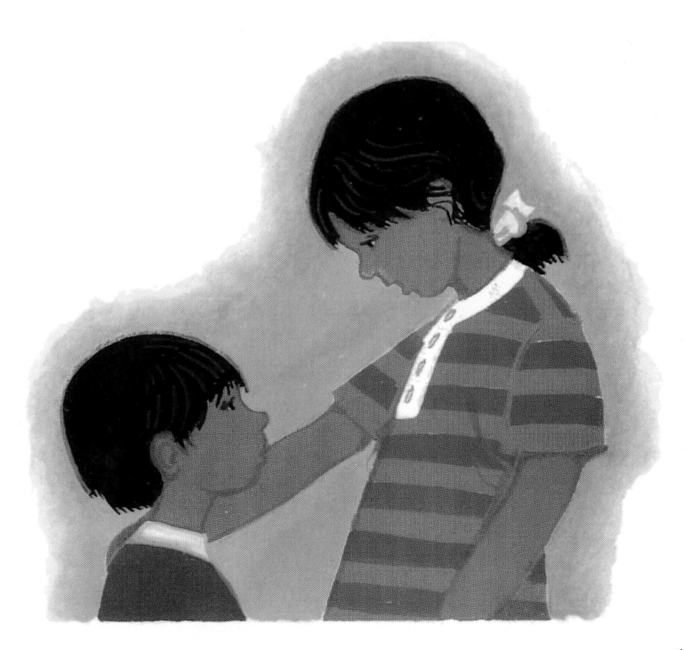

Then I saw a great big, happy smile spread across my brother's face. He was looking at something behind me. I didn't even have to ask what it was.

**Nothing else could make my brother
look that happy. It had to be—a dog!**

I tried. I tried very hard.

I shut my eyes and pretended the dog wasn't there.

I took deep breaths so my heart wouldn't beat so fast.

I clenched my hands so they would stop trembling.

I prayed the dog would go away.

Then I felt its feet upon my shoulders. I thought of sharp claws.

I felt its rough, wet tongue against the back of my neck. I thought of all those teeth.

That did it!

I couldn't get into the house fast enough! Across the yard I ran. I yanked open the screen door and quickly slammed it shut. I even hooked it.

Safe behind the door, I stood, catching my breath.

Then I went to the window. I knew what I would see.

Yes, there was my brother, with his arms around that dog.

I watched them play together. I watched them for a long time.

I suppose that dog would have played with me, too, if I had been outside.

But I stayed inside.
I felt bad about it, but I stayed inside.
Oh well, everybody's afraid of
something, I guess.

My Brother Is Afraid Of Just About Everything

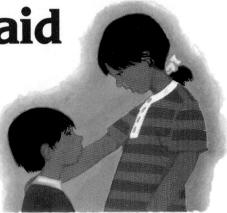

Meet the Author

Lois Osborn was a teacher for 26 years. She started writing after she retired. She likes to visit schools to read her books and talk about writing.

Meet the Illustrator

Loretta Krupinski began drawing as a very young child and has never stopped. She has created marine paintings of boats and lighthouses for many years. Recently, she began illustrating and writing children's picture books. Krupinski enjoys going back and forth between real-life marine paintings and children's picture books.

Theme Connections

Talk About It

Everybody is afraid of something. Here are some things to talk about:

- What is the little brother afraid of in this story?
- What is his older sister afraid of?
- Are you afraid of any of those things?
- Name some fears that many people have.
- How could you help someone who is afraid?

Look at the Concept/Question Board. Are there any questions on it that you can answer now? Do you have any new questions about being afraid? Write the questions on the Board. Maybe the next reading will help answer your questions.

Record Ideas

 Draw a line down the center of a page in your Writing Journal. On the left side of the page, make a list of three things you know of that people are afraid of. On the right side of the page, write what you could do to overcome each fear.

Share a Story

Think of a story about someone you know who was afraid of something. Share the story with a group of your classmates.

Goblin Story

by Else Holmelund Minarik
illustrated by Maurice Sendak

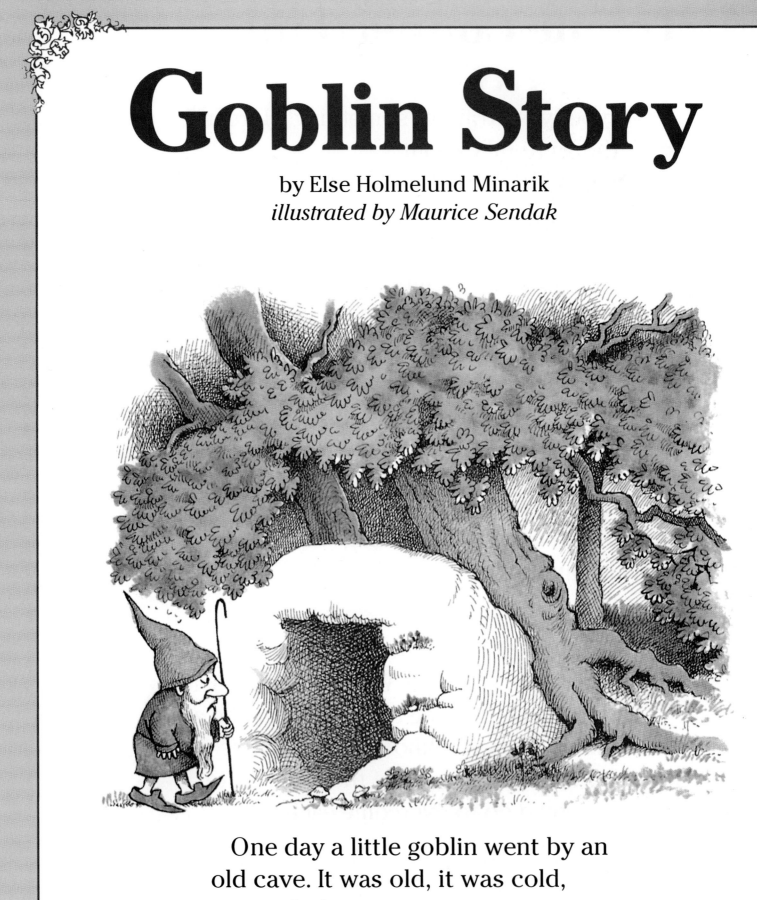

One day a little goblin went by an
old cave. It was old, it was cold,
it was dark.

And something inside it went bump.
What was that?
BUMP!
"Hoo–ooh—" cried the goblin.

He got so scared that he jumped
right out of his shoes. Then he
began to run.

Pit–pat–pit–pat–pit–pat—
What was that? SOMETHING
was running after him.

Oh my goodness, what could it be?
The goblin was too scared to look
back. He ran faster than ever.
But so did the SOMETHING that
went pit–pat–pit–pat–pit–pat—

The goblin saw a hole in a tree.
He jumped inside to hide.
The pit–pat–pit–pat came closer,
closer—CLOSER—till it stopped,
right by the hole in the tree!

Then all was quiet.
Nothing happened.
Nothing.

The little goblin wanted to peek out.
It was so quiet.
Should he peek out?

Yes, he would. He WOULD peek out!
And he did.

"Eeeeeh—!" cried the goblin.
Do you know what he saw?

He saw—his SHOES!
His own little shoes—
and nothing more.

"Goodness," said the goblin,
hopping out of the tree.

"That old bump in the cave made me jump right out of my shoes. But they came running after me, didn't they! And here they are!"

He picked up his shoes, hugged
them, and put them back on.

"Good little shoes," said the goblin.
"You didn't want to stay behind,
did you!" He laughed.

"Who cares about an old bump,
anyway," he said.

So he snapped his fingers,
and skipped away—
just like that!

Goblin Story

Meet the Author

Else Holmelund Minarik was born in Denmark and moved to the United States with her family when she was four years old. She became interested in writing for children after she became a first grade teacher. There were times when she couldn't find enough books for her students, so she decided to write some books herself.

Meet the Illustrator

Maurice Sendak knew he wanted to be a writer and illustrator even before he went to school. When he was old enough to have a job, he helped create comic strips every day after school. He grew up to write and illustrate many books, including *Where the Wild Things Are*. The monsters in this story remind Maurice of his aunts and uncles.

Theme Connections

Talk About It

In this story, a goblin is being chased by something. At first it is scary, but it ends up being funny. Here are some questions to talk about:

- What makes the story scary in the beginning?
- Why is the story funny in the end?

Look at the Concept/Question Board. Are there any questions on it that you can answer now? Do you have any new questions about being afraid? Write the questions on the Board. Maybe the next reading will help answer your questions.

Record Ideas

 Did you have any ideas about what might be following the goblin? Write your ideas in your Writing Journal. Pick one thing and describe it. Make it scary.

Draw a Picture

In your Writing Journal draw a picture of the goblin looking afraid. Draw a scary thing in a thought cloud above his head.

Something Is There

Lilian Moore
illustrated by Toni Goffe

Something is there
　　there on the stair
　　　　coming down
　　　　　　coming down
　　　　　　　　stepping with care.
　　　　　　Coming down
　　　　　　　　coming down
　　　　　　　　　　slinkety-sly.
Something is coming and wants to get by.

Strange Bumps

by Arnold Lobel

Owl was in bed. "It is time to blow out the candle and go to sleep," he said with a yawn.

Then Owl saw two bumps under the blanket at the bottom of his bed. "What can those strange bumps be?" asked Owl.

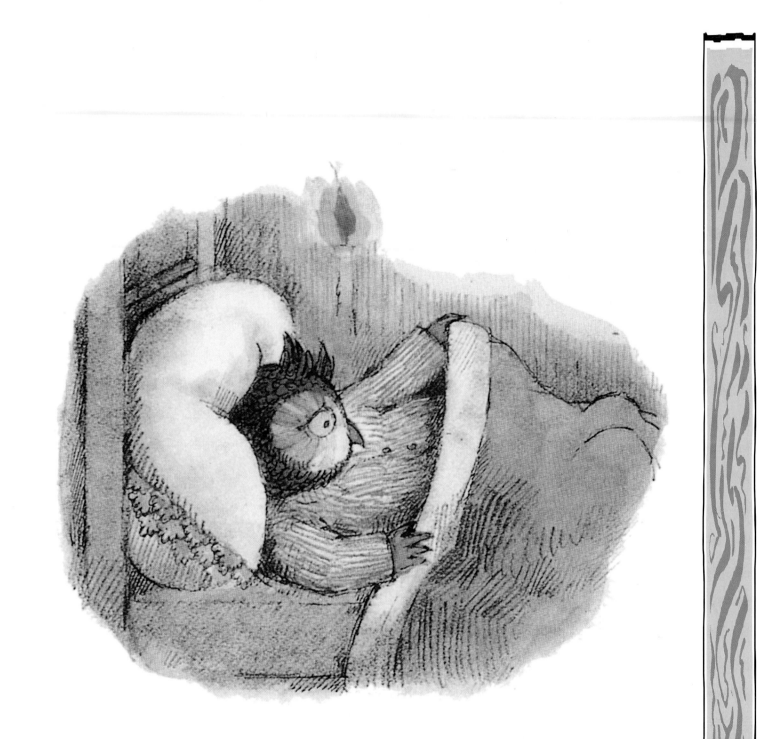

Owl lifted up the blanket. He looked
down into the bed. All he could see
was darkness. Owl tried to sleep, but
he could not.

"What if those two strange bumps grow bigger and bigger while I am asleep?" said Owl. "That would not be pleasant."

Owl moved his right foot up and down. The bump on the right moved up and down. "One of those bumps is moving!" said Owl.

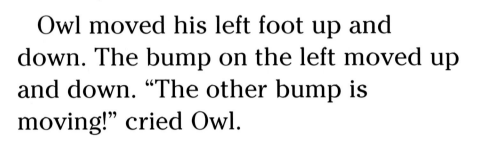

Owl moved his left foot up and
down. The bump on the left moved up
and down. "The other bump is
moving!" cried Owl.

Owl pulled all of the covers off his bed. The bumps were gone. All Owl could see at the bottom of the bed were his own two feet.

"But now I am cold," said Owl. "I will cover myself with the blankets again."

As soon as he did, he saw the same two bumps.

"Those bumps are back!" shouted Owl. "Bumps, bumps, bumps! I will never sleep tonight!"

Owl jumped up and down on top of his bed.

"Where are you? What are you?" he cried. With a crash and a bang the bed came falling down.

Owl ran down the stairs. He sat in his chair near the fire.

"I will let those two strange bumps sit on my bed all by themselves," said Owl. "Let them grow as big as they wish. I will sleep right here where I am safe."

And that is what he did.

Strange Bumps

Meet the Author and Illustrator

Arnold Lobel was born in Los Angeles, California. When he was a child, he often told stories and drew pictures to go with these stories to amuse his classmates. He would also put on his own plays at home. Lobel studied at an art college, then he began his career in children's books. He wrote and illustrated more than 100 books.

Theme Connections

Talk About It

In the story, Owl tries to find out what the strange bumps are. He should have figured it out. Here are some things to talk about:

- What did Owl do to try to find out what the bumps were?
- Why was Owl afraid?
- Have you ever been afraid of something at bedtime? What did you do?
- Why is this story funny?

Look at the Concept/Question Board and answer any questions that you can. Do you have any new questions about being afraid? Write them on the Board. Maybe the next reading will help answer your questions.

Record Ideas

 In your Writing Journal draw something that might make a strange shape in your room at night. Then write three things that you might think as you look at this strange shape.

Change the Story

Think about what might have happened if Owl had discovered what the "strange bumps" were. Rewrite the ending of the story.

FINE Art

Cat trying to catch a goldfish. c. 1838–1840. **Utagawa Kuniyoshi.** Color woodcut. Philadelphia Museum of Art, gift of Mrs. John D. Rockefeller.

The Gulf Stream. 1899. **Winslow Homer.** Oil on canvas.
$28\frac{1}{8} \times 49\frac{1}{8}$ in. The Metropolitan Museum of Art, Catharine
Lorillard Wolfe Collection, Wolfe Fund, 1906 (06.1234).
Photograph ©1995 The Metropolitan Museum of Art.

His First Lesson. 1903. **Frederic Remington.** Oil on canvas.
Amon Carter Museum, Fort Worth, Texas. 1961.231.

Little Miss Muffet

Nursery Rhyme

illustrated by Dominic Catalano

Little Miss Muffet sat on her tuffet,
Eating her curds and whey;
Along came a spider and sat down beside her
And frightened Miss Muffet away.

Clyde Monster

Robert L. Crowe

illustrated by Kay Chorao

Clyde wasn't very old, but he was growing—uglier every day. He lived in a large forest with his parents.

Father Monster was a big, big monster and very ugly, which was good. Friends and family usually make fun of a pretty monster. Mother Monster was even uglier and greatly admired. All in all, they were a picture family—as monsters go.

Clyde lived in a cave. That is, he was supposed to live in a cave, at night anyway. During the day, he played in the forest, doing typical monster things like breathing fire at the lake to make the steam rise.

He also did typical Clyde things like turning somersaults that made large holes in the ground, and generally bumping into things. He was more clumsy than the average monster.

At night, Clyde was supposed to go to his cave and sleep. That's when the trouble started. He refused to go to his cave.

"Why?" asked his mother. "Why won't you go to your cave?"

"Because," answered Clyde, "I'm afraid of the dark."

"Afraid," snorted his father until his nose burned. "A monster of mine afraid? What are you afraid of?"

"People," said Clyde. "I'm afraid there are people in there who will get me."

"That's silly," said his father. "Come, I'll show you." He breathed a huge burst of fire that lit up the cave. "There. Did you see any people?"

"No," answered Clyde. "But they may be hiding under a rock and they'll jump out and get me after I'm asleep."

"That is silly," pointed out his mother with her pointed tongue. "There are no people here. Besides, if there were, they wouldn't hurt you."

"They wouldn't?" asked Clyde.

"No," said his mother. "Would you ever hide in the dark under a bed or in a closet to scare a human boy or girl?"

"Of course not!" exclaimed Clyde, upset that his mother would even think of such a thing.

"Well, people won't hide and scare you either. A long time ago monsters and people made a deal," explained his father. "Monsters don't scare people, and people don't scare monsters."

"Are you sure?" Clyde asked.

"Absolutely," said his mother. "Do you know of a monster who was ever frightened by a people?"

"No," answered Clyde after some thought.

"Do you know of any boys or girls who were ever frightened by a monster?"

"No," he answered quickly.

"There!" said his mother. "Now off to bed."

"And no more nonsense about being scared by people," ordered his father.

"Okay," said Clyde as he stumbled into the cave. "But could you leave the rock open just a little?"

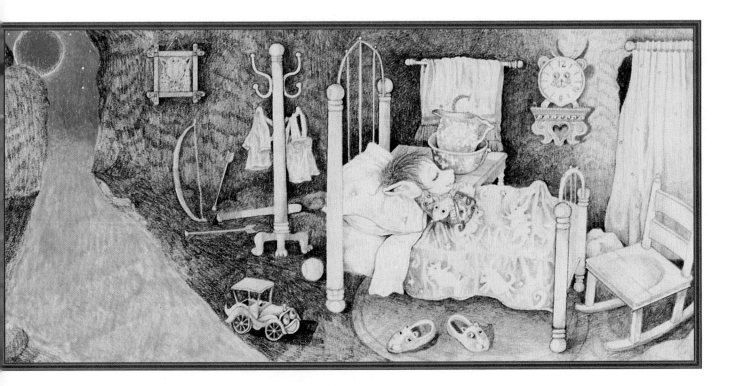

Clyde Monster

Meet the Author

Robert L. Crowe used to teach. Then he became a superintendent of schools. He wrote "Clyde Monster" to help his own children overcome their fear of the dark.

Meet the Illustrator

Kay Chorao is from Indiana. Now she lives in New York City. As a child, Kay loved to draw. As soon as she was old enough to hold a crayon, she "scribbled drawings over every surface," including the breakfast room table!

Theme Connections

Talk About It

Here are some questions to help you:

- What was Clyde Monster afraid of?
- How did his parents help him?
- Have you ever felt that way?
- How did another person help?

Look at the Concept/Question Board. Are there any questions on it that you can answer now? Do you have any new questions about being afraid? Write the questions on the Board. Maybe the next reading will help answer your questions.

Record Ideas

 In your Writing Journal, write words to describe how you feel when you are afraid in the dark. Make a title for your list.

Describe a Character

Clyde Monster was described at the beginning of the story. Goblin, Owl, and Little Miss Muffet were not described in their stories. Choose one of these characters and make up a description. Include information about what they look like, how they feel, and what they like to do.

The Cat and the Mice

Aesop
retold by Margaret Clark
illustrated by Charlotte Voake

A family of mice was being chased every day by a hungry cat.

"What are we going to do?" said Mother, as they all sat around her one evening.

Everyone had something to suggest, but the smallest mouse said, "If we hang a bell around his neck, then we shall hear him coming and we'll have time to get out of his way."

All the mice squealed in excitement and told the smallest mouse how clever he was.

Then the oldest mouse in the family spoke. "That may *sound* like a good idea," he said, "but tell me: which one of you is brave enough to go up to the cat and hang a bell around his neck?"

187

The Cat and the Mice

Meet the Author

Margaret Clark started to write when her children were young. As they grew, she changed the age levels of her stories. She says, "I write for young people and of course for myself. Most of my books grow out of my own experiences." Margaret likes to write about things she has done, like camping.

Meet the Illustrator

Charlotte Voake always wanted to be an illustrator. She won a poster contest when she was twelve. Voake published her first book while she was still in college. She lives in England and enjoys sailing when she isn't drawing.

Theme Connections

Talk About It

The smallest mouse has an idea that some of the other mice think is a good one. Here are some things to talk about:

- Why does the oldest mouse think the smallest mouse's idea is not a good one?
- What might happen if the mouse tried to hang the bell on the cat's neck?
- Should the mice be afraid? Why?
- What are some things you should be afraid of?

Look at the Concept/Question Board and answer any questions that you can. Do you have any new questions about being afraid? Write them on the Board. Maybe the next reading will help answer your questions.

Record Ideas

 Draw a big lightbulb in your Writing Journal. In it write the ideas you and your group had for what the mice could do with the cat.

Add to the Story

Discuss which idea each child in your group liked best and why.

Bibliography

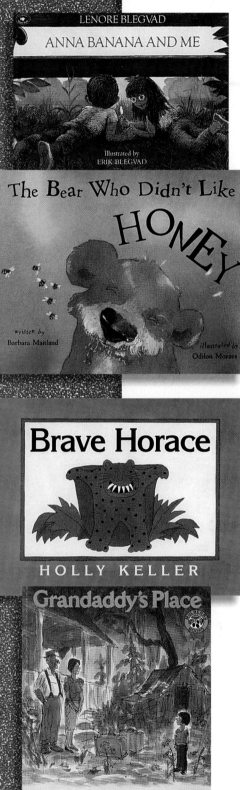

Anna Banana and Me

by Lenore Blegvad. Find out how Anna helps her friend to be brave.

The Bear Who Didn't Like Honey

by Barbara Maitland. Why is Little Bear always telling fibs? Is there something he's afraid of?

Brave Horace

by Holly Keller. How does Horace find the nerve to go to a monster party? Would you be scared?

Grandaddy's Place

by Helen V. Griffith. Janetta's afraid of the animals on Grandaddy's farm. How can she lose her fear?

Hattie and the Fox

by Mem Fox. What happens when Hattie the Hen finds a fox in the bushes?

I Hear a Noise

by Diane Goode. What happens when a monster gets scared and needs his mother?

Storm in the Night

by Mary Stolz. On a dark and stormy night, Grandfather tells Thomas about another storm long ago.

We're Going On a Bear Hunt

by Michael Rosen. Join a fearless family as they go bear hunting. What will they find?

Homes

Are all homes alike? Would a good home for a bunny be a good home for a bird or a crab? What makes a good home for all the different people and animals in the world?

Homes Around the World

by Deborah Eaton

Argentina

Lesotho, South Africa

The Philippines

Here you will see many homes and many faces in many different far-off places.

Cliff houses are cool
when the sun is hot.

Mali

It's not too
hot here.
Grass grows
on a roof.

Germany

195

A reed hut is made of dried plants.

Peru

You need a ladder to get to some pueblo houses.

New Mexico, USA

Flowers make this home pretty.

Austria

196

Their house is up on stilts.

The Philippines

His house has a tin roof.

Poland

197

Trailers are homes on wheels.

Nevada, USA

Some homes float.

Hong Kong

198

Some homes fold right up.

Morocco

People can even turn palm leaves into a home.

Guatemala

A porch is a
nice place
to sit.

Thailand

A fireplace warms a home.

New Mexico, USA

Doors are for friends coming in.

China

Windows let light in and let people smile out.

Argentina

201

Big and tall . . .

Indonesia

Round and small . . .

Somalia

All over the world, homes are for living . . .

Sudan

and homes are for enjoying.

Utah, USA

Homes Around the World

Meet the Author and Photographer

Deborah Eaton decided to become a writer when she was sixteen years old. She has written *No One Told the Aardvark the Elephants Are Coming*, *Where Is My Baby?*, and *The Family Tree*. Eaton lives in Maine and has a cat named Pudge who sits in the window and waves at people as they pass by the house. Eaton loves to write about animals and is working on a new book.

Theme Connections

Talk About It

Homes are usually well suited to the environment and culture in that part of the world. No matter how homes look, their purpose is always to provide shelter for those who live in them. Here are some things to talk about:

- How are the homes in the pictures different?
- How are they the same?
- Why do the homes look so different?

Look at the Concept/Question Board. Are there any questions on it that you can answer now? Do you have any new questions about homes? Write the questions on the Board. Maybe the next reading will help answer your questions.

Record Ideas

 Put your best ideas in your Writing Journal. Use a list or a chart.

Building a House

by Byron Barton

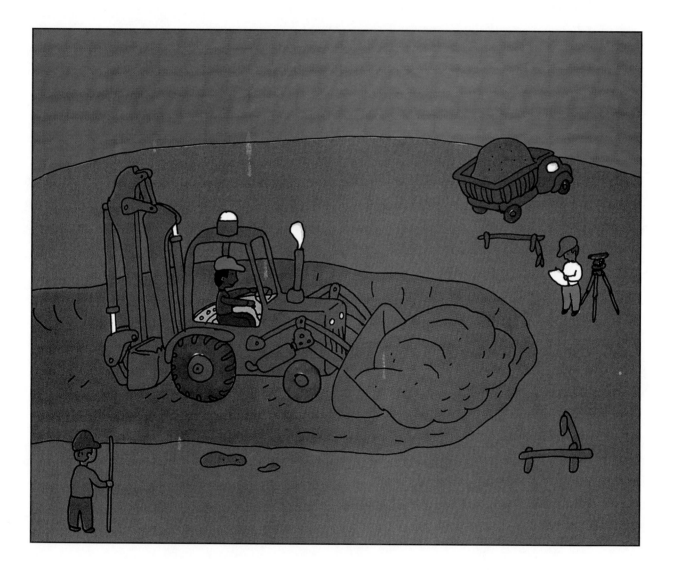

On a green hill a bulldozer digs
a big hole.

Builders hammer
and saw.

A cement mixer
pours cement.

Bricklayers lay large
white blocks.

Carpenters come and make a wooden floor.

They put up walls.

They build a roof.

A bricklayer builds a fireplace and a chimney too.

A plumber puts in pipes for water.

An electrician wires for electric lights.

Carpenters put in windows and doors.

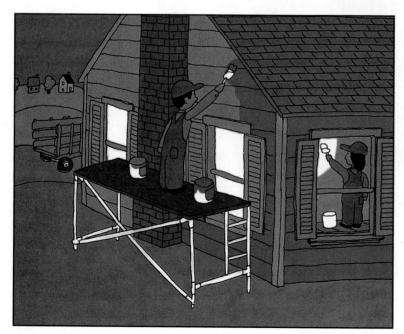

Painters paint inside and out.

The workers leave.

The house is built.

The family moves inside.

Building a House

Meet the Author and Illustrator

Byron Barton became known as "the artist" in grade school. He got the name because he often painted pictures. He said, "My pictures were hanging all over the back walls of the class." He grew up to write and illustrate stories about how to do things like build a house, put together dinosaur bones, and travel on a spaceship.

Theme Connections

Talk About It

Many people must work together to build a house. It is very important that houses are built well by people who are skilled. Here are questions to help talk about the story.

- Why does it take so many people to build one house?
- How long does it take to build a house?
- Who builds houses?
- What do people use to build a house?

Look at the Concept/Question Board and answer any questions that you can. Do you have any new questions about homes? Write them on the Board. Maybe the next reading will help answer your questions.

Record Ideas

 List in your Writing Journal the different people who work together to build a house.

Make a Booklet

Copy three sentences from the story on pieces of paper. Illustrate each one. Put the papers in order. Staple the pages together in the correct order.

The Three Little Pigs

*retold and illustrated
by Margot Zemach*

Long ago, three little pigs lived happily with their momma pig. But the day came when their momma told them it was time for them to go out into the world.

"Build good, strong houses,"
she said, "and always watch out
for the wolf. Now goodbye,
my sons, goodbye."

As the first little pig was going along, he met a man who was gathering straw.

"Please, sir," he said, "give me some straw to build me a house."

So the man gave him some straw
and the first little pig built himself
a house.

One day the wolf came knocking
at his door.

"Little pig, little pig," he called.
"Let me come in!"

But the first little pig said:
"No, no, I won't let you in—
not by the hair of my chinny-chin-chin."

"Well then," said the wolf,
"I'll huff and I'll puff and I'll blow
your house down."
So he huffed and he puffed
and he blew the house down,
and he ate up the first little pig.
Yumm-yum!

As the second little pig was going along, he met a man with a load of sticks.

"Please, sir," he said, "give me
some sticks to build me a house."
So the man gave him some sticks
and the second little pig built
himself a house.

One day the wolf came knocking
at his door.

"Little pig, little pig," he called.
"Let me come in!"

But the second little pig said:
"No, no, I won't let you in—
not by the hair of my chinny-chin-chin."

"Well then," said the wolf,
"I'll huff and I'll puff
and I'll blow your house down."
So he huffed and he puffed
and he huffed and he puffed
and he blew the house down,
and he ate up the second little pig.
Yumm-yum!

As the third little pig was going along, he met a man with a load of bricks.

"Please, sir," he said, "give me some bricks to build me a house."

So the man gave him some bricks
and the third little pig built himself
a good, strong house.

One day the wolf came knocking
at his door.
"Little pig, little pig," he called.
"Let me come in!"
But the third little pig said:
"No, no, I won't let you in—
not by the hair of my chinny-chin-chin."

"Well then," said the wolf,
"I'll huff and I'll puff
and I'll blow your house down."
So he huffed and he puffed
and he huffed and he puffed . . .
and he huffed and he puffed,
but he just <u>couldn't</u> blow the
house down!

This made the wolf angry, but he only said, "Little pig, I know where there's a field of turnips."

"Oh, where?" asked the third little pig.
"Right down the road," said the wolf.
"I'll come for you at ten o'clock
tomorrow morning, and we'll
go together."

The next morning the little pig got up at nine o'clock and hurried to the turnip field. He was back safe in his house when the wolf came knocking.

"Little pig," said the wolf. "It's time to go."

"Oh, I already got myself a nice basket of turnips," the little pig said.

This made the wolf very angry,
but he just said,
"Little pig, I know where there's
a big apple tree."

"Oh, where?" asked the little pig.

"Across the meadow," said
the wolf.
"I'll come for you tomorrow at
nine o'clock. We'll go together."

The next morning the little pig got up at eight o'clock. He was busy picking apples when he saw the wolf coming.

"Here's an apple for you!" the little pig called, and he threw it so far the wolf had to chase after it. Then the little pig climbed down and ran away.

As soon as the little pig was safe in his house, the wolf came knocking.

"Little pig," he said, "tomorrow there's going to be a fair in town. I'll come for you at eight o'clock."

The next morning the little pig got up at seven o'clock and hurried to the fair, where he had a good time, until he saw the wolf coming. The little pig jumped into a barrel to hide. But the barrel fell over and rolled down the hill, faster and faster, straight toward the wolf— and it knocked him down!

The little pig was cooking himself a big pot of soup when the wolf came banging on his door. "Little pig," he called, "I didn't see you at the fair."

"Oh, but I saw you," said the little pig. "I was riding home in the barrel that knocked you down."

This made the wolf really angry, much angrier than before.

"Little pig!" he roared. "I've had enough of your tricks. Now I'm coming to get you." The wolf leaped onto the little pig's roof and he threw himself down the little pig's chimney, and he fell right into the pot of soup and was cooked.

That night, the third little pig
had wolf soup for supper.
Yumm-yum!

The Three Little Pigs

Meet the Author and Illustrator

Margot Zemach's mother was an actress. She traveled a lot, so Margot lived with her grandparents in Oklahoma. "I have always drawn pictures, all my life," she says. Her daughter, Kaethe, is also an artist.

Theme Connections

Talk About It

One purpose of a home is protection from weather and from others. Different climates require different materials for building a house.

- What are some things that can be used to build houses?
- What would you use to build a house?
- Why didn't the first pig build his house of bricks?
- Why did the third pig build his house of bricks?

Look at the Concept/Question Board. Are there any questions on it that you can answer now? Do you have any new questions about homes? Write the questions on the Concept/Question Board. Maybe the next reading will help answer your questions.

Record Ideas

 Put your best ideas in your Writing Journal. Use a list or a chart.

Make a House

Choose something to build a house with like straws, blocks, or paper. Write why your house might or might not fall down.

Animal Homes

by Illa Podendorf

Many animals make their homes on top of the ground.

Cottontail rabbits make nests in fields in the spring.

Baby rabbits in nest

A cottontail's nest is warm. It is made from soft grass and lined with fur. The mother lines the nest with fur from her own body.

In winter, cottontails do not live in nests. Then they live under a barn or under some corn stalks.

Mice

Sometimes white-footed mice make their nests among plants on top of the ground.

A fox does not do much building to make its home. It finds a hollow log or a hole among the rocks and makes its den there.

Fox cubs in their den

Squirrel nest

Some animal homes are above the ground.

Sometimes squirrels make nests of twigs and leaves and grass in branches of trees.

Other times squirrels make homes in holes in trees. These homes are usually their winter homes.

Squirrel

Raccoons live near water in woods.
Some raccoons make their homes in
hollow trees.

Raccoon nest

A garden spider lives among plants. A garden spider spins a web. It stays on or near its web.

Spiderweb

Some animal homes are under the ground.

Ground squirrels build homes under the ground.

Their home is a long hall. This hall is called a tunnel. Sometimes the ground squirrels leave a pile of dirt at the door to their home.

Ground squirrel

Badgers live underground, too. If you
look for them, it is easy to see where
they dig their tunnels.

Badger den

Skunks often make their homes in holes in the ground. They sometimes dig new holes. But they may use a hole that some other animal has made. Sometimes skunks crawl under buildings and make their homes there.

Skunk nest

Some kinds of ants build their homes underground. They dig on and on until they have a long tunnel underground.

Ants digging a tunnel

Ants make more than one tunnel. At
the end of each tunnel they make a
room. In an ant home there are many
tunnels and many rooms.

Nursery

Queen's Chamber

Storeroom
for food

Ant nest

The first room to be made is a nursery. The baby ants live here.

Many of the rooms are storerooms for food. The worker ants bring back food to put in the storerooms.

Ants carrying food to the storeroom

Beaver lodge

Some animal homes are in water. Beavers build their homes in water. A beaver's home has a big room above water. The door to the home is underwater. A beaver swims underwater and up into the room of his home.

Beaver

Sunfish make a nest at the bottom of a pond. The father brushes a place clean with his fins. Then the mother fish lays her eggs. They both protect the nest from their enemies.

Sunfish

Woodchuck burrow

Chickadee nest

Remember, animals live in many places.
Some animals live in the ground.
Some animals live high above the ground.
Some animals live in water.
Other animals live on land.

Alligator and turtles

Elk

Deer

Horned toad

Some animals live in the woods.
Others live on the desert.
Some kinds of animals build
unusual homes.
Each animal home is just right for
the animal that builds and lives in it.

Spittlebug home

Hornet nest

Animal Homes

Meet the Author

Illa Podendorf was a science teacher and wrote science books for children. She believed that students should be creative and should be able to solve problems.

Theme Connections

Talk About It

The type of home an animal lives in depends on that animal's needs. Animals make their homes in places that best suit their needs. Talk about these questions:

- Why don't all animals live in the same kind of home?
- Why don't all animals just live outside?
- Where are some places animals live?
- What animal homes have you seen?

Look at the Concept/Question Board and answer any questions that you can. Do you have any new questions about homes? Write them on the Board. Maybe the next reading will help answer your questions.

Record Ideas

 Put your best ideas in your Writing Journal. Use a list or a chart.

Make a Picture

Draw a picture of a place where other animals live, like a park or a forest. Then, draw some animals' homes on your picture. Write the name of the animal beside the home you drew for it.

FINE Art

Part Two of My Village, in Yorubaland, Nigeria, Africa. c. 1980–1990. **Chief Z. K. Oloruntoba.** Plant dyes on fabric. Collection of the artist. Photo: Suzanne Kaufman.

Shacks. 1919. **Lawren Harris.** Oil on canvas, 107.9 × 128 cm. National Gallery of Canada, Ottawa, Ontario, Canada.

Street Scene-Gloucester. c. 1940.
Edward Hopper. Oil on canvas.
Edwin and Virginia Irwin Memorial
Collection, Cincinnati Art Museum.

Making Tent for Winter. 1974.
Malaya Akulukjuk. Stencil print
by Solomon Karpik, Pangnirtung
Print Shop, 1975. Canadian
Museum of Civilization.

**Miniature funerary model of a
house.** Han dynasty, 202 BC–AD 220.
Chinese. Pottery. Musée Cernuschi,
Paris. Photo: Giraudon/Art Resource, NY.

259

Make a Home

Nancy Pemberton

illustrated by Barbara Bruno

You can make a home for worms.
You will need:
- a big glass jar with a wide mouth
- loose soil
- pebbles mixed with soil
- earthworms
- lettuce and cornmeal for the worms to eat
- black paper and tape

1. Fill the bottom of the jar with pebbles mixed with soil. Add loose soil to fill most of the jar. Keep the soil moist.

2. Put small pieces of lettuce and some cornmeal on top of the soil.

3. Dig up some earthworms and put them in the jar.

4. Tape black paper to the sides of the jar for one week. That will make the worms tunnel near the glass.

5. Take off the black paper.
Watch how the worms
move and eat.

6. When you are done
watching the worms,
return them to their
outdoor home.

Make a Home

Meet the Illustrator

Barbara Bruno is a writer, artist, and photographer. She has illustrated stories in many books and magazines.

Theme Connections

Talk About It

All animals, including worms, are accustomed to building or finding their own homes and we should respect that whenever possible. Talk about the following questions.

- Why put the worms outside after you have looked at them?
- Where do you find worms?
- Why do you put black paper on the jar?

Look at the Concept/Question Board and answer any questions that you can. Do you have any new questions about homes? Write them on the Board. Maybe the next reading will help answer your questions.

Record Ideas

 Put your best ideas in your Writing Journal. Use a list or chart.

Make a Home

Make a home for worms like you see in the book. Ask for help to read the instructions and to get everything you need.

Home for a Bunny

Margaret Wise Brown

illustrated by Garth Williams

"Spring, Spring, Spring!" sang the frog.

"Spring!" said the groundhog.

"Spring, Spring, Spring!" sang the robin.

It was Spring.

The leaves burst out.

The flowers burst out.

And robins burst out of their eggs.

It was Spring.

In the Spring a bunny came down the road.
He was going to find a home of his own.
A home for a bunny,
A home of his own,
Under a rock,
Under a stone,
Under a log,
Or under the ground.
Where would a bunny find a home?

"Where is your home?"
he asked the robin.

"Here, here, here," sang the robin.
"Here in this nest is my home."

"Here, here, here," sang the little robins
who were about to fall out of the nest.
"Here is our home."

"Not for me," said the bunny.
"I would fall out of a nest.
I would fall on the ground."
So he went on looking for a home.

"Where is your home?" he asked the frog.

"Wog, wog, wog," sang the frog.

"Wog, wog, wog,

Under the water,

Down in the bog."

"Not for me," said the bunny.
"Under the water, I would drown in a bog."
So he went on looking for a home.

"Where do you live?" he asked the
groundhog.

"In a log," said the groundhog.

"Can I come in?" said the bunny.

"No, you can't come in my log,"
said the groundhog.

So the bunny went down the road.
Down the road and down the road he went.
He was going to find a home of his own.
A home for a bunny,
A home of his own,
Under a rock
Or a log
Or a stone.

Where would a bunny find a home?
Down the road
and down the road
and down the road
he went, until—

He met a bunny.
"Where is your home?"
he asked the bunny.
"Here," said the bunny.

"Here is my home.
Under this rock,
Under this stone,
Down under the ground,
Here is my home."

"Can I come in?" said the bunny.
"Yes," said the bunny.
And so he did.
And that was his home.

Home for a Bunny

Meet the Author

Margaret Wise Brown was born in New York City. She wrote about 100 books for children, as well as songs. She did not have many friends when she was a child, and she spent lots of time "in the woods and along the beaches and in the imaginary countries of the worlds I made up."

Meet the Illustrator

Garth Williams was born in New York City. Both of his parents were artists. Garth remembers that when he was growing up, "Everybody in my house was always either painting or drawing, so I thought there was nothing else to do in life but make pictures."

Theme Connections

Talk About It

All animals need homes for shelter and protection, but their homes look different and are in different places. Here are some things to talk about:

- Why is the bunny looking for a home?
- What kind of home does the bunny need?
- Why was it hard for the bunny to find a home?
- Do you think the bunny chose the right place? Why or why not?

Look at the Concept/Question Board. Are there any questions on it that you can answer now? Do you have any new questions about homes? Write the questions on the Board. Maybe the next reading will help answer your questions.

Record Ideas

 Put your best ideas in your Writing Journal. Use a list or a chart.

Make a Map

Draw a map of the path that bunny took. Show the animals that bunny met. Write what the animals said to each other.

The Rabbit Warren

Marie Aubinais

illustrated by Monique Félix

The baby rabbits are born
in a burrow underground.

Their mother has prepared a nest of fur for them. And each morning she feeds her babies.

Then she closes the nest and goes out to eat.

When the baby rabbits are a bit older,
they move into their parents' burrow.

Their parents live close to other rabbit families. All of the burrows together are called a warren.

The rabbits go to the bathroom in
a special place outside their burrows.

Each morning and evening the rabbits go out to eat. When it is nice and safe outside, they take a walk.

If any rabbit senses danger, it warns its family by thumping the ground very hard with its hind legs.

When a rabbit is chased, it quickly
runs back to the safety of its burrow.

But when it is calm, the rabbits move around in small groups and eat grass, roots, and greens.

And whenever a rabbit gets its paws
wet, it licks them dry.

The Rabbit Warren

Meet the Author

Marie Aubinais has always been interested in magazines and children's books. In 1984, she began working on a magazine for children 3–7 years old. She later began writing on a different magazine, for children 8–12 years old. Other books by Marie Aubinais: *The Farm, The Jungle, Birds* and *The Sea.*

Meet the Illustrator

Monique Félix has written and illustrated many children's books. She was born in Switzerland, where she later studied graphic arts at an art school. Her stories and illustrations are enjoyed by children all around the world.

Theme Connections

Talk About It

Rabbits live together as a family and families live together as a community. They use their homes for protection and safety.

- How are rabbit homes like people's homes?
- Why do you think rabbits like to live so close together?
- What is a rabbit warren?
- How do rabbits warn other rabbits of danger?

Look at the Concept/Question Board. Are there any questions on it that you can answer now? Do you have any new questions about homes? Write the questions on the Concept/Question Board. Maybe the next reading will help answer your question.

Record Ideas

 Put your best ideas in your Writing Journal. Use a list or a chart.

Make a Painting

Make a painting of a rabbit warren. Show how rabbits live together.

Is This a House for Hermit Crab?

Megan McDonald

illustrated by S. D. Schindler

Hermit Crab was forever growing too big for the house on his back. It was time to find a new house. He crawled up out of the water looking for something to hide in, where he would be safe from the pricklepine fish.

He stepped along the shore, by the sea, in the sand . . . *scritch-scratch, scritch-scratch* . . . until he came to a rock.

Is this a house for Hermit Crab?

Turning himself around, Hermit Crab backed his hind legs beneath the rock. The rock would not budge. It was too heavy.

So he stepped along the shore, by
the sea, in the sand . . . *scritch-scratch,
scritch-scratch* . . . until he came to a
rusty old tin can.

Is this a house for Hermit Crab?

When he tried to walk with the can on his back, it bumped and clunked. It was too noisy.

So he stepped along the shore, by the sea, in the sand . . . *scritch-scratch, scritch-scratch* . . . until he came to a piece of driftwood.

Is this a house for Hermit Crab?

Hermit Crab crawled deep in
the rounded hollow at one end.
too dark.

So he stepped along the shore, by the
sea, in the sand . . . *scritch-scratch,
scritch-scratch* . . . until he came to a
small plastic pail.

Is this a house for Hermit Crab?

Climbing up toward the rim, *oops!* he fell right in. He clawed, and he clawed, until he climbed back out. It was too deep.

So he stepped along the shore, by the sea, in the sand . . . *scritch-scratch, scritch-scratch* . . . until he came to a nice round hole in the sand.

Is this a house for Hermit Crab?
He poked his head down into the opening. A huge pair of eyes blinked back at him. Hermit Crab shivered as he scurried away from the big fiddler crab peering out of its burrow. It was too crowded.

So he stepped along the shore, by the sea, in the sand . . . *scritch-scratch, scritch-scratch* . . . until he came to a fishing net.

Is this a house for Hermit Crab?

Poking his claws into the heap, he got tangled and caught. Hermit Crab wriggled and wriggled until he found his way out of the net. It had too many holes.

So he stepped along the shore, by the sea, in the sand . . . *scritch-scratch, scritch-scratch.* . . . All of a sudden a gigantic wave tossed and tumbled pebbles and sand over Hermit Crab's head. He swirled and whirled with the tide and was washed back out to sea.

Sleeker than a shark, the pricklepine fish darted out from its hiding place in the tall seaweed. Every spine on its back stood straight as a steeple. Mouth open wide, it headed right for Hermit Crab. Hermit Crab raced across the ocean floor . . . *scritch-scritch-scritch-scritch* . . . scurrying behind the first creature he saw.

It was a sea snail, and he hoped it would hide him, but the shell was empty.

The shell was empty!

Hermit Crab scrambled inside as quick as a flash, and clamped his claw over the opening in the shell.

The pricklepine fish circled the snail shell three times, but he could not catch sight of the crab he had been chasing. He glided off in search of something else to eat.

When all seemed still and quiet, Hermit Crab snuggled comfortably

down into his new shell. It was not too heavy, not too noisy, not too dark, and not too deep. It was not too crowded and did not have too many holes.

At last, Hermit Crab had found a new home. And it fit just right.

Is This a House for Hermit Crab?

Meet the Author

Megan McDonald remembers growing up in "a house stuffed with books." She was the youngest of five girls, and they all liked to read books and tell stories, so there were always interesting dinnertime storytelling sessions. "As a writer, I try to tell stories that will invite children to re-establish a connection with themselves and their own imagination."

Meet the Illustrator

S. D. Schindler studied to become a doctor, but decided he wanted to be an artist instead. He enjoyed drawing when he was very young, and especially liked drawing animals. He was known as the class artist in school.

Theme Connections

Talk About It

It is important for all animals to have a home that provides shelter and protection. Even though all animals need a home, not all types of homes are suitable for animals. Here are some questions to talk about:

- Why did Hermit Crab need a new house quickly?
- Why did it take Hermit Crab so long to find a new house?
- Why do you think Hermit Crab didn't build a house?
- What was wrong with the house Hermit Crab tried before the shell?

Look at the Concept/Question Board. Are there any questions about homes that you can answer now? Do you have any new ones to put on the Board?

Record Ideas

 Put your best ideas in your Writing Journal. Use a list or a chart.

Make a Sign

Make a sign to try and sell a home. Draw a picture of the home you want to sell, and write some words that tell why someone should buy it. Put a price on the home.

Bibliography

The Big Orange Splot

by Daniel Pinkwater. What would a house that looked like your dreams be like? Visit Mr. Plumbean's street of dreams.

Evan's Corner

by Elizabeth Starr Hill. Evan finds a place of his own in his crowded house. How does Evan make his corner special?

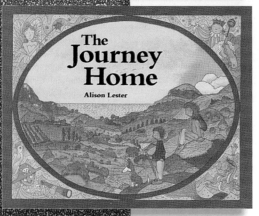

My House, Mi Casa: A Book in Two Languages

by Rebecca Emberley. This is a book that has pictures of household objects with captions in both English and Spanish.

The Journey Home

by Alison Lester. Where do Wild and Woolly end up when they dig a huge hole in their Australian sandpit? How do they get home?

Mouse Mess

by Linnea Riley. Do you clean up after yourself? Does Mouse?

My House Has Stars

by Megan McDonald. Find out what all the houses in the world have in common when night falls.

Our Home is the Sea

by Riki Levinson. A young boy rushes home from school through the streets of Hong Kong. Why is he in such a hurry?

To Market, To Market

by Anne Miranda. What does Miranda bring home from the market that makes her kitchen a disaster area?

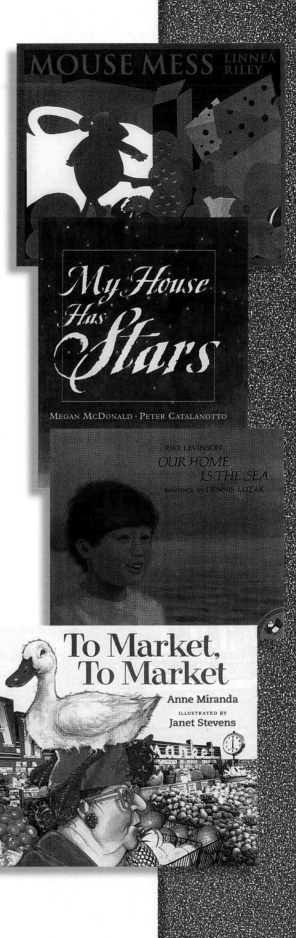

310

Glossary

A

absolutely (ab´ sə lōōt´ lē) *adv.* Without any doubt; for certain.

admired (ad mīrd´) *adj.* Well thought of.

average (av´ ər ij) *adj.* Ordinary; like most others.

awhile (ə hwīl´) *adv.* For a length of time.

B

batter (bat´ ər) *n.* Flour, milk, eggs, and sugar mixed together to make a cake.

boa constrictor (bō´ ə kən strik´ tər) *n.* A snake that kills its prey by squeezing.

bog (bog) *n.* A swamp; a marsh.

bog

311

breathe (brēth) *v.* To take air in and blow air out.

bricklayer (brik´ lā´ ər) *n.* A person who builds walls out of bricks or concrete blocks.

budge (buj) *v.* To move a little bit.

builder (bil´ dər) *n.* A person who builds or makes things, such as houses.

bulldozer (bool´ dō´ zər) *n.* A large machine that a person rides like a tractor while the machine pushes stones, dirt, and trees out of the way.

burrow (bûr´ ō) *n.* A hole or tunnel under the ground that an animal digs to live in.

burst (bûrst) *n.* A small, quick explosion. *v.* To come out suddenly and strongly.

C

calm (käm) *adj.* Still; quiet; peaceful.

carpenter (kär´ pən tər) *n.* A person who makes things out of wood.

cement (si ment´) *n.* A mixture of sand, water, and crushed stone that dries as hard as stone.

clamp (klamp) *v.* To hold tightly.

claw (klô) *n.* 1. A sharp, curved nail on an animal's foot. 2. The hard, pincher part at the end of a crab's or lobster's legs. *v.* To scratch or pull up by using hands, nails, or claws.

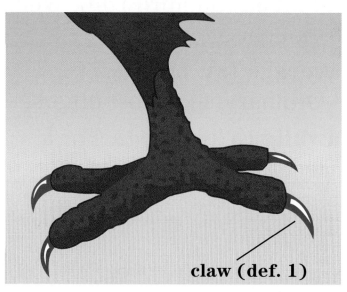

claw (def. 1)

clench (klench) *v.* To close tightly.

clever (klev´ ər) *adj.* Smart.

clumsy (klum´ zē) *adj.* Likely to trip or bump into things.

clunk (klungk) *v.* To hit hard; to make a loud noise.

couch (kouch) *n.* A wide, soft chair; a sofa.

cozy (kō´ zē) *adj.* Snug; comfortable.

crash (krash) *v.* To fall and hit the ground hard.

curd (kûrd) *n.* Soft cheese; the lumps in cottage cheese.

D

dandelion (dan´ də lī´ ən) *n.* A weed that has a bright yellow flower.

dash (dash) *v.* To run quickly.

den (den) *n.* A wild animal's home.

den

desert (dez´ ərt) *n.* A large area of very dry land.

driftwood (drift´ wŏŏd´) *n.* A piece of wood floating in the water or washed up onto a beach.

droop (drōŏp) *v.* To bend or curve down.

drown (droun) *v.* To die from being kept under water and not able to breathe air.

E

eager (ē´ gər) *adj.* Excited about doing something.

electrician (i lek trish´ ən) *n.* A person who puts electrical wires in a building.

enemy (en´ ə mē) *n.* Someone who wants to hurt another.

engineer (en´ jə nēr´) *n.* The person who drives a train.

enormous (i nor´ məs) *adj.* Very big.

exclaim (ik sklām´) *v.* To say something suddenly and loudly.

F

fiddler crab (fid´ lər krab´) *n.* A small, round shellfish with one claw larger than the others.

flop (flop) *v.* To fall suddenly.

forest (for´ ist) *n.* A large area of trees.

forest

frightened (frīt´ nd) *adj.* Afraid; scared.

G

gather (gath´ ər) *v.* To collect; to bring together.

generally (jen´ ər ə lē) *adv.* Most of the time.

gigantic (jī gan´ tik) *adj.* Very big; huge.

gnarled (närld) *adj.* Twisted and lumpy.

goblin (gob´ lin) *n.* A very tiny, make-believe person who often gets into trouble.

grain (grān) *n.* The seed of a plant like wheat.

ground (ground) *n.* The earth; dirt. *v.* Crushed into a powder.

H

hare (hâr) *n.* A gray or brown animal that looks like a large rabbit.

hare

hind (hīnd) *adj.* At the back.

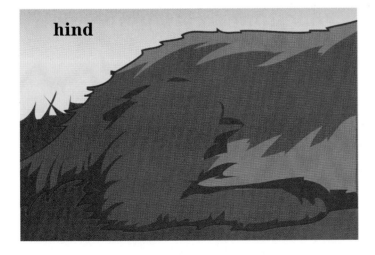

hind

hoe (hō) *v.* To dig in the soil with a garden tool.

hollow (hol′ ō) *n.* A hole; an empty space. *adj.* Empty inside.

huge (hūj) *adj.* Very large.

J

joke (jōk) *n.* Something that won't ever work.

junk (jungk) *n.* Something that is not worth anything; trash.

L

laugh (laf) *v.* To make a sound that shows something is funny.

laughter (laf′ tər) *n.* The sound a person makes when something is funny.

lightning (līt′ ning) *n.* A flash of electricity across the sky.

Pronunciation Key: at; lāte; câre; fäther; set; mē; it; kīte; ox; rōse; ô in bought; coin; bŏŏk; tōō; form; out; up; ūse; tûrn; ə sound in about, chicken, pencil, cannon, circus; chair; hw in which; ring; shop; thin; th^{ere}; zh in treasure.

M

meadow (med´ ō) *n.* An open field covered with grass and wildflowers.

meadow

mend (mend) *v.* To sew up holes; to fix by sewing.

mill (mil) *n.* A place where workers grind grain into flour.

mill

moist (moist) *adj.* A little wet; damp.

N

nonsense (non´ sens) *n.* Foolishness; silliness.

nursery (nûr´ sə rē) *n.* A room set apart for young animals or babies.

P

pace (pās) *n.* The speed of walking or running.

pair (pâr) *n.* Two things that are alike or almost alike.

pebble (peb´ əl) *n.* A small stone.

peek (pēk) *v.* To look quickly.

peer (pēr) *v.* To look at something as if studying it.

perhaps (pər haps´) *adv.* Maybe.

picture (pik´ chər) *n.* A perfect example.

pleasant (plez´ ənt) *adj.* Nice.

plod (plod) *v.* To walk slowly and heavily.

plumber (plum´ ər) *n.* A person who puts water pipes into a building.

porch (porch) *n.* A covered entrance on the front or back of a house, like a room with a roof but no walls.

prepare (pri pâr´) *v.* To make ready; to plan.

protect (prə tekt´) *v.* To keep safe.

pueblo (pweb´ lō) *n.* A group of houses built on top of each other, made of stone or adobe bricks.

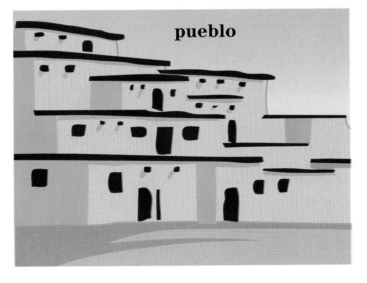
pueblo

Q

quite (kwīt) *adv.* Very.

quiver (kwiv´ ər) *v.* To shake; to tremble; to shiver.

R

reed (rēd) *n.* The stiff stem of a grassy plant.

refuse (ri fyoōz´) *v.* To say no to something.

reply (ri plī´) *v.* To answer; to say.

ripe (rīp) *adj.* Fully grown; ready for eating.

S

scamper (skam´ pər) *v.* To run lightly or playfully.

scramble (skram´ bəl) *v.* To crawl quickly.

scurry (skûr´ ē) *v.* To run quickly.

sense (sens) *v.* To come to know.

shade (shād) *v.* To give cover from the sun.

shall (shal) *v.* Will.

shiver (shiv´ ər) *v.* To shake because of fear.

shout (shout) *v.* To call loudly.

sleek (slēk) *adj.* Smooth.

smack (smak) *v.* To hit.

snooze (snooz) *v.* To sleep for a short time; to doze; to take a nap.

snort (snort) *v.* To blow air noisily through the nose.

somersault (sum´ ər sôlt´) *n.* A turn that is made by rolling head over heels.

somersault

spine (spīn) *n.* A stiff, sharp fin on the back of a fish.

spine

squeal (skwēl) *v.* To make a loud, high cry.

stalk (stôk) *n.* The stem of a plant.

steam (stēm) *n.* A mist that rises from boiling water.

steeple (stē´ pəl) *n.* A tall, pointed top on a tower or church.

stilt (stilt) *n.* A pole or a long stick that holds something up.

stilt

swirl (swûrl) *v.* To spin around quickly.

swirl

stomach (stum′ ək) *n.* The middle part of a person's body.

straw (strô) *n.* The dried stems of plants.

stroll (strōl) *v.* To walk slowly.

stumble (stum′ bəl) *v.* To walk in a clumsy way.

suggest (səg jest′) *v.* To tell an idea; to give a plan.

supposed to (sə pōzd′ to͞o) *v.* Expected to.

T

tend (tend) *v.* To take care of; to watch over.

thirsty (thûr′ stē) *adj.* Needing something to drink.

thud (thud) *n.* A sound made when something falls.

thump (thump) *v.* To beat.

thunder (thun′ dər) *n.* A loud noise heard after lightning.

thunderstorm (thun′ dər storm′) *n.* A storm with thunder and lightning.

Pronunciation Key: **a**t; lāte; cȃre; fäther; s**e**t; mē; **i**t; kīte; **o**x; rōse; ô in b**ou**ght; c**oi**n; b**ook**; t**oo**; f**o**rm; **ou**t; **u**p; ūse; tûrn; ə sound in **a**bout, chick**e**n, penc**i**l, cann**o**n, circ**u**s; **ch**air; **hw** in **wh**ich; ri**ng**; **sh**op; **th**in; **th**ere; **zh** in trea**s**ure.

tide (tīd) *n.* The rise and fall of the sea.

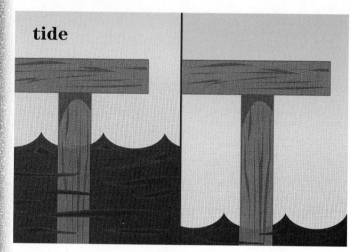

tide

tin (tin) *n.* A kind of metal.

tired (tīrd) *adj.* Sleepy.

tongue (tung) *n.* Part inside the mouth that helps a person talk.

tortoise (tor´ təs) *n.* A large land turtle.

tortoise

tough (tuf) *adj.* Strong.

tower (tou´ r) *v.* To be much taller than.

tremble (trem´ bəl) *v.* To shake; to shiver.

tuffet (tuf´ it) *n.* A low seat.

turnip (tûr´ nip) *n.* A vegetable with a large, round root that is eaten.

turnip

typical (tip´ i kəl) *adj.* Usual; the regular kind.

U

ugly (ug´ lē) *adj.* Not pleasant looking.

unusual (un yōō′ zhōō əl) *adj.* Strange; rare; different from most others.

usually (yōō′ zhōō əl ē) *adv.* Most of the time.

V

vacuum (vak′ yōōm) *v.* To clean with a machine that picks up dirt.

vine (vīn) *n.* A plant that has a very long stem. A vine can grow along the ground or up a wall.

vine

W

warren (wor′ ən) *n.* A place where many rabbits live.

wheat (hwēt) *n.* A plant that has seeds that can be eaten or made into flour.

wheat

whey (hwā) *n.* The part of milk that becomes like water when milk is being made into cheese.

Pronunciation Key: at; l**ā**te; c**â**re; f**ä**ther;
s**e**t; m**ē**; **i**t; k**ī**te; **o**x; r**ō**se; ô in b**ou**ght; c**oi**n;
b**oo**k; t**oo**; f**o**rm; **ou**t; **u**p; **ū**se; t**û**rn; ə sound
in **a**bout, chick**e**n, penc**i**l, cann**o**n, circ**u**s;
chair; hw in **wh**ich; ri**ng**; **sh**op; **th**in; t**h**ere;
zh in trea**s**ure.

whirl (hwûrl) *v.* To spin
around quickly.

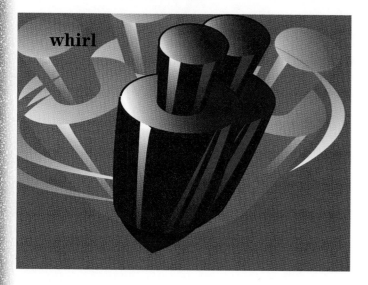

whirl

wriggle (rig´ əl) *v.* To twist; to
squirm.

Y

yank (yangk) *v.* To pull
quickly and hard.

Acknowledgments, continued

Photo Credits

10(tl), ©Hilarie Kavanagh/Tony Stone Images; **10(br)**, ©Leonard Lee Rue/Photo Researchers, **Inc.**; **134**, ©Olan Mills; **182(t)**, © Merle Fox Photography; **194(tl)** Robert Frerck/The Stock Market; **194(tr)** ©Nicholas DeVore/Tony Stone Images; **194(br)**, ©Blair Seitz/Photo Researchers, Inc.; **195(b)**, ©Focus/Moller/Woodfin Camp & Associates; **195(t)**, ©Wolfgang Kaehler/Corbis; **196(t)**, ©Robert Frerck/Woodfin Camp & Associates, **196(bl)**, ©Dan Budnik/Woodfin Camp & Associates; **196(br)**, ©Adam Woolfitt/Woodfin Camp & Associates; **197(t)**, ©Traveler's Resource/Tony Stone Images, **197(b)**, ©Momatiuk/ Eastcott/Woodfin Camp & Associates; **198(t)**, ©Harry Gruyaert/Magnum Photos, Inc., **198(b)**, ©Porterfield/Chickering/Photo Researchers, Inc.; **199(t)**, ©Craig Aurness/Woodfin Camp & Associates; **199(b)**, ©David Hiser/Tony Stone Images; **200(t)**, ©Hilarie Kavanagh/Tony Stone Images; **200(b)**, ©David Stoecklein/The Stock Market; **201(t)** ©Paul Chesley/National Geographic Society Image Collection; **201(b)**, ©John F. Mason/The Stock Market; **202(t)**, ©Charles & Josette Lenars/Corbis; **202(b)**, ©Mike Yamashita/Woodfin Camp & Associates; **203(t)**, ©Martin Rogers/Tony Stone Images; **203(b)**, ©E. Spiegelhalt/Woodfin Camp & Associates; **204**, ©Nicholas DeVore/Tony Stone Images; **240**, ©Oxford Scientific Films/Animals Animals; **241**, ©Dwight R. Kuhn/DRK Photo; **242**, ©Leonard Lee Rue/Photo Researchers, Inc.; **243(t)**, ©PHOTRI; **243(b)**, ©Oxford Scientific Films/Animals Animals; **244**, ©W. Perry Conway/Tom Stack & Associates; **245**, ©John Gerlach/Tom Stack & Associates; **246**, ©Alan G. Nelson/Dembinsky Photo Associates; **247**, ©W. Perry Conway/Tom Stack & Associates; **248**, ©Ernest Wilkinson/Animals Animals; **249**, ©Doug Wechsler/Animals Animals; **251**, ©Jeff Foott/DRK Photo; **252(t)**, ©Dominique Braud/Tom Stack & Associates, **252(b)**, ©Wendy Shattil/Bob Rozinski/Tom Stack & Associates; **253**, ©E.R. Degginger/Photo Researchers, Inc.; **254(tl)**, ©E.R. Degginger/Animals Animals, **254(tr)**, ©John Gerlach/Animals Animals; **254(bl)**, ©Carl R. Sams, II/Dembinsky Photo Associates; **254(br)**, ©Stan Osolinski/Dembinsky Photo Associates; **255(tl)**, ©Stephen J. Krasemann/Photo Researchers, Inc., **255(bl)**, ©E.R. Degginger/Animals Animals, **255(tr)**, ©David T. Roberts/Nature Images, Inc./Photo Researchers, Inc., **255(br)**, ©Richard Kolar/Animals Animals; **256**, ©W. Perry Conway/Tom Stack & Associates; **278(t)**, ©Morgan Collection/Archive Photos.

Unit Opener Illustrations

12–13 G. Brian Karas; **114–115** Lisa McCue; **196–197** Loretta Krupinski